a guide to

CORNWALL

by

WEEKEND JOURNALS

WORDS
Milly Kenny-Ryder

DESIGN
Simon Lovell

PHOTOGRAPHY
Gabriel Kenny-Ryder

weekendjournals.co.uk

CONTENTS

—

Our chosen places take you on a journey from Launceston travelling anticlockwise around the Cornish coast.

PREFACE

—

There's something special about Cornwall. Perhaps it's the light, the blissful isolation, the evidence of a mysterious past or just the dramatic coastline. Spending extended periods of time exploring this enchanted county allowed us to meet many of the locals and become attuned to their slower pace of life. The shops have eccentric opening times based around the tides and the surf, and the restaurant kitchens close when the daily catch has all gone - it feels refreshing and healthy to live this way.

There are many celebrated places to visit time and time again in Cornwall, and I know frequent visitors often have a favourite beach or ice-cream shop they eagerly return to every trip. For us, it is the magical cloutie tree at Madron Wishing Well or a pasty from Philps after a bracing dip in the sea. I hope you will be encouraged to venture further afield to the exciting and special venues we have discovered, sometimes in the most unlikely corners...

Although much of Cornwall's appeal is nostalgic, there are innovators who are bringing modern, stylish but sympathetic ideas to the Cornish scene: boutique hotels for hip travellers, gastronomic eateries for keen foodies and contemporary galleries and gardens to satisfy discerning aesthetes.

Put simply, there is so much more to experience in Cornwall than initially meets the eye, and I hope this book will inspire you to see and do more while visiting.

Milly Kenny-Ryder

MAP OF CORNWALL

St Ives

Penzance

Porthle

Porthcurno

Isles of Scilly

Launceston

Port Isaac

Polzeath

Padstow

Bodmin

Newquay

St Austell

Looe

Truro

Falmouth

St Mawes

elston

COOMBESHEAD FARM

—

Hotel & Restaurant

Lewannick, Launceston, PL15 7QQ
01566 782 009
coombesheadfarm.co.uk

Just five minutes drive from the Devon-Cornwall border, Coombeshead Farm is ideal as a weekend break from London. Set up by Pitt Cue Co owner Tom Adams and Michelin-starred chef April Bloomfield, it is a foodie destination with beautiful bedrooms as a bonus. Set amongst sixty-six acres of meadows and woodland, this guesthouse and working farm has a peaceful atmosphere that encourages you to feel at home.

The Georgian Farmhouse has been designed by Ali Childs, of Studio Alexandra, who has thoughtfully juxtaposed rustic and retro countryside memorabilia with modern features and luxurious amenities. At dinnertime guests can enjoy a friendly supper at the communal dining table, cooked by Tom or a guest chef and featuring produce from the farm. Picnics can also be provided for lunchtime jaunts on the scenic Coombeshead land.

ST TUDY INN

—

Restaurant

St Tudy, Bodmin, PL30 3NN
01208 850 656
sttudyinn.com

Emily Scott is an ambitious and optimistic chef, who took over this inn determined to offer locals and visitors great food in a delightful setting. The charming Cornish pub is situated in St Tudy, a quaint village in North Cornwall. After extensive redecoration, the pub feels cosy and welcoming with Nicole Heidaripour prints on the walls and vintage worn furniture.

All Emily's cheffing experience has been put to good use in the kitchen, where seasonality and local produce reign. The menu is full of comforting classics with a twist, fish and chips for example is upgraded to the irresistibly tasty Monkfish tails in rosemary focaccia crumb with fries and citrus mayo. St Tudy Inn runs regular events, including Pig and Cider nights with a hog roast and regional ales.

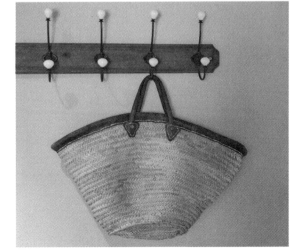

CAMEL VALLEY

—

Vineyard

Nanstallon, Bodmin, PL30 5LG
01208 779 59
camelvalley.com

When the sun shines on the Bodmin valleys they compete with the most picturesque fields in the world. The lush and verdant vineyards in this area sometimes appear more similar to the Californian wine region.

The South West is receiving more and more recognition for its refined wine varieties. Camel Valley is one of Cornwall's oldest established, and largest wine producers with a celebrated sparkling and a collection of reds, whites and rosés. The excellent soil and sunny climate encourage full-flavoured grapes.

This glorious setting is the perfect place to enjoy a tasting flight or just a glass of the flagship fizz 2013 'Cornwall' Brut. Alternatively take a tour of the vineyards, to truly understand the scale and beauty of the place. If you wish to enjoy the location for longer there are two tranquil cottages on site to rent.

RESTAURANT NATHAN OUTLAW

—

Restaurant

6 New Road, Port Isaac, PL29 3SB
01208 880 896
nathan-outlaw.com

A veritable prodigy of the kitchen, Nathan Outlaw worked under Gary Rhodes and Rick Stein before establishing his own reputation, opening the first two Michelin-star fish restaurant in the world. It is a clean, stylish dining room in Port Isaac with sharp service and immaculate seafood dishes.

Outlaw's food is blissfully minimalist, he aims 'to take ingredients away from the plate rather than add' which allows the Cornish produce, always cooked to perfection, to shine. The four course set lunch features delights such as Gurnard with Porthilly Sauce, one of Outlaw's most elegant and brilliant recipes. If you can't secure a table at the fine dining eatery, head to Port Isaac's charming harbour, where Nathan has opened his more relaxed Fish Kitchen, also to Michelin acclaim.

SURFSIDE

—

Restaurant

On the Beach, Polzeath, PL27 6TB
01208 862 931
surfsidepolzeath.com

Surfside is an exciting venture from London-based mixologist Tristan Stephenson, author of The Curious Bartender and part of the drinks company Fluid Movement who founded Purl and The Whistling Shop bars in London. Surfside has become a local hit, serving fresh food and cocktails at the water's edge in Polzeath. Located on a corner of the beach, the restaurant is only accessible via the sand which adds to the experience.

Although the venue appears casual from the exterior, inside the offerings are for serious foodies with surf and turf platters and inventive cocktails. Thanks to the isolated location Surfside feels intimate and exclusive, with panoramic sea views adding something special to the meal.

PADSTOW BREWING COMPANY

—

Brewery

The Brewery, 4a Trecerus Estate, Padstow, PL28 8RW
01841 532 169
padstowbrewing.co.uk

An industrial park on the outskirts of Padstow is the home of Padstow Brewing Company. The award-winning, independent microbrewery offers a boutique range of artisan beers and ciders, bottled stylishly and available for visitors to buy. The husband and wife team, Caron and Des Archer, began brewing in early 2013, testing out different equipment and recipes in an old surf-shower.

After establishing a successful recipe and method, Padstow Brewing Company became a professional enterprise and proceeded to win numerous awards. The company has since expanded and now supplies some of the best foodie venues in Cornwall. Craft beer enthusiasts can enjoy a tour with tasting or an immersive brewing experience to fully understand the unique process.

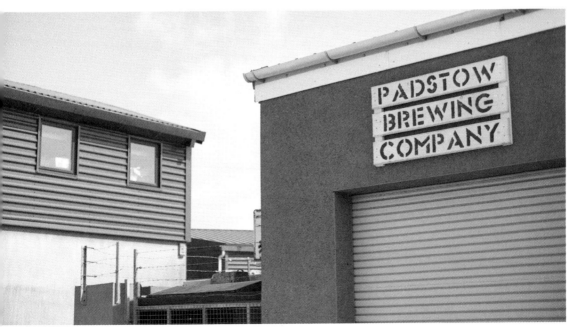

PAUL AINSWORTH AT NO.6

—

Restaurant

6 Middle Street, Padstow, PL28 8AP
01841 532 093
paul-ainsworth.co.uk

Housed within a historic Georgian Townhouse on a quaint Padstow street, Paul Ainsworth at No. 6 is the chef's most prestigious restaurant. The playful and creative dishes showcase Cornwall's finest seasonal ingredients while hinting at his varied culinary influences. The restaurant has a cosy and relaxed feel, with a private dining room for special occasions. At lunchtime a set menu allows guests to sample his signature flavours at a very reasonable price. Paul Ainsworth's nostalgic 'Taste of the Fairground' dessert has received particular recognition and is a favourite on the menu.

For more casual cuisine visit the chef's bistro Rojano's in the Square, also in Padstow and just a few minutes walk away.

TREVIBBAN MILL & APPLETON'S
AT THE VINEYARD
—
Vineyard & Restaurant

Dark Lane, near Padstow, PL27 7SE
01841 541 413
trevibbanmill.com

Situated on the slopes of the Issey brook near Padstow, Trevibban Mill is one of the newer Cornish wineries but is already producing award-winning wines. Liz and Engin began planting in 2008 with an ambition to produce top quality Cornish wines and ciders. Native sheep graze on the land and their wool is for sale in the vineyard shop. Tours and tastings can be arranged to sample a range of the different wine and cider varieties.

Also on site is Appleton's at the Vineyard, where ex-Fifteen head chef Andy Appleton is managing the kitchen, feeding hungry visitors with fine Italian dishes showcasing the local produce. Choose from a beautiful piece of sustainable fish, or a bowl of comforting pasta. The dishes provide the ideal accompaniment to a glass of Trevibban Mill wine.

THE SCARLET

—

Hotel

Tredragon Road, Mawgan Porth, Newquay, TR8 4DQ
01637 861 800
scarlethotel.co.uk

Perched on the rugged clifftops overlooking Mawgan Porth, The Scarlet Hotel is the ultimate eco retreat. A rare, adults-only establishment in Cornwall, The Scarlet is an instantly calming place in which to spend time. It features fresh contemporary bedrooms, many of which boast private garden terraces or balconies, and an exemplary restaurant with seasonal dishes by chef Tom Hunter.

The hotel proudly allows dogs in some rooms for a small fee per night, or if you fancy a bit of exercise on the beach, you can borrow the hotel dog, the ideal walking companion. Downstairs, the destination spa offers Ayurvedic treatments to nourish the body and soul and a soothing Relaxing Room with hanging cocoon pods for post-treatment sleeps. Rest in the outdoor sauna or soak in the Clifftop Hot Tub which offers dramatic views across the Atlantic.

FIFTEEN

—

Restaurant

On The Beach, Watergate Bay, Newquay, TR8 4AA
01637 861 000
fifteencornwall.co.uk

The Cornish outpost of Jamie Oliver's successful chef training programme has an optimum position on the beach at Watergate Bay. This popular restaurant nurtures young talent, while offering a range of flavoursome Italian dishes. The menu features Mediterranean favourites and the selection of homemade pastas and seasonal desserts are the highlight.

Suitable for all occasions, the bistro style restaurant has a modern interior with plenty of natural light flooding in through the large sea-facing windows, making the most of the spectacular location. The award-winning restaurant operates as a registered charity, with all profits going to the Cornwall Food Foundation.

WATERGATE BAY HOTEL

—

Hotel

On The Beach, Watergate Bay, Newquay, TR8 4AA
01637 860 543
watergatebay.co.uk

Watergate Bay Hotel in North Cornwall, is set on one of the area's most spectacular beaches. With two miles of golden sand and an impressive swell from the Atlantic, it is a popular destination for surfers; dolphins are also often spotted jumping through the azure sea. The hotel has light and laid-back double rooms, family suites and bunk rooms to choose from, making it suitable for both romantic getaways and family holidays. The décor is fresh and modern with splashes of colour and seaside artwork that reminds guests of their coastal location.

Downstairs, a stylish Swim Club offers an indoor infinity pool and private rooms for luxurious spa treatments. Food options are plentiful, including brasserie-style dining at Zacry's, and Jamie Oliver's Fifteen on site for Italian cuisine.

CHAPTER 1

—

Restaurant

8 Morfa Hall, Cliff Road, Newquay, TR7 1SG
01637 499 263
chapter1restaurant.co.uk

Newquay is very popular with student visitors but many would ignore it as a Cornish holiday destination, though the scenic coastline attracts many keen surfers. Chapter 1 is an unlikely culinary treat in this town, the first solo venture from promising young chef, Tom Mackins. Previously he has worked for legendary chefs Kevin Viner and Paul Ainsworth and proved his talent by opening Chapter 1 aged just 26.

Refined and beautiful, Tom's plates of food are carefully constructed elevating the simplest ingredients through clever techniques and a passion for juxtaposing intense flavours. Try to visit when the six-course tasting menu is on offer, it is good value and the perfect opportunity to witness this creative chef's expertise and creativity. Tom's innovative recipes have been included in various cookbooks and his reputation is growing steadily beyond Cornwall.

TREVOSE HARBOUR HOUSE

—

Hotel

22 The Warren, St Ives, TR26 2EA
01736 793 267
trevosehouse.co.uk

St Ives is the most popular town to visit in Cornwall, with a beautiful coastline and many cultural highlights. Located in the centre of town, Angela and Olivier Noverraz reopened Trevose Harbour House in 2013 after a full restoration with six stylish bedrooms that feel fresh and suit the seaside surroundings. In the summer months a suntrap terrace is a lovely place to relax and in winter the cosy living room has an open fireplace and an honesty bar. Angela and Olivier take pride in the breakfast they provide: a feast of organic continental delights and an array of nourishing hot breakfast dishes.

For the best views of the harbour, book the rooftop suite, a glorious bedroom and bathroom decorated with hints of mid-century design whilst providing every luxury you could need. For something more private, Sands Studio is the latest project from the couple, a stunning seaside guesthouse located in the fashionable Downalong area of St Ives.

BARBARA HEPWORTH MUSEUM
AND SCULPTURE GARDEN
—
Museum

Barnoon Hill, St Ives, TR26 1AD
01736 796 226
tate.org.uk

Nestled amongst tropical shrubs and exotic flowers stand the solemn sculptures of Barbara Hepworth, Cornwall's leading lady.

The Trewyn Studios appear as if untouched since Hepworth ended her days here in 1975 and the workshop and intimate garden have a quiet, peaceful atmosphere. Sheltered from the fierce coastal winds, it is a fertile oasis, especially in spring when the blossom is out. The garden is particularly enchanting early in the morning before all the tourists arrive.

St Ives has a long history as a home for major artists, potters and sculptors, but Barbara Hepworth is undoubtedly the most prolific and potent.

THE BLACK ROCK

—

Restaurant

Market Place, St Ives, TR26 1RZ
01736 791 911
theblackrockstives.co.uk

St Ives boasts some of Cornwall's most exciting culinary establishments, and also holds an annual food festival on the beach. Many of the successful restaurants in this seaside town boast beautiful beach views and al fresco opportunities.

Black Rock is less advantageously placed, but more than compensates with its sophisticated, contemporary cuisine. This stylish eatery is a family project, and proprietors Emma and David Symons are the fourth generation to work on these premises, transforming the space into a restaurant in 2008. The couple are clearly passionate about offering good quality local, seasonal food and welcoming service.

David leads the kitchen in an endeavour to create dishes, which are both delicious and affordable, using the freshest seafood, and meat from local farms. Recipes like homemade gnocchi with wild mushrooms and soft egg prove the team are just as dexterous with vegetables. Emma looks after the restaurant, an attractively decorated room with a changing display of artwork and pottery, and vintage signs adorning the walls.

PLUMBLINE

—

Shop

2 Barnoon Hill, St Ives, TR26 1AD
07703 797 060
plumblinestives.co.uk

Plumbline is a discreet design shop worth seeking out. The small space is perfectly curated - a pristine gallery for stylish shoppers wishing to discover something exceptional.

Deborah, the imaginative owner, handpicks items from a variety of talented artists from all over the country. Plumbline's stock is a stark contrast to the seaside memorabilia that fills the more touristy shops. Jochen Holz, the East London glassblower has a range of his striking work here as well as elegant ceramics by Sam Hall. It is very evident that Plumbline champions local artisan makers and craftsmen as in Jennie Hancox's lovely jewellery collection.

Behind the shop there is a small good-looking flat for visitors to rent; a design haven for the aesthetically inclined traveller.

HIDDEN KITCHEN

—

Restaurant

The Masonic Lodge, St. Andrews Street, St Ives, TR26 1AH
07792 639 755
hiddenkitchenstives.co.uk

Hidden Kitchen is a supper club and culinary concierge serving unique food to its St Ives clientele. Located on the corner of St. Andrews Street, in the centre of the historic town, it is easy to miss this understated dining room. Chef James Watson and his wife Georgina worked together in the catering business before opening their first venue. The intimate dining experience in the boutique restaurant makes it feel like a dinner party at a friend's house.

James regularly plays host to visiting chefs who provide diners with constantly changing, exciting international cuisines. Guest chefs have included Gordon Ramsay student Lee Skeet and Japanese cook Naoko Kashiwagi. After the meal leave a message to show your appreciation on the blackboard tables.

PORT OF CALL

—

Shop

9 Market Place, St Ives, TR26 1RZ
01736 796 211
academyandco.com

Port of Call is the third retail space from Kate and James Deseta, a brother and sister team who are bringing clean aesthetics and a love of design to St Ives.

The carefully displayed homeware items and magazines are sure to induce domestic envy. The shop stocks niche brands such as Haeckels skincare from Margate and Parisian stationer's Papier Tigre alongside a pretty selection of house plants and accessories. Stock up on speciality journals or pick up an inspiring travel book.

Nearby, their clothing store, Academy & Co stocks diverse designers like Norse Projects and Ally Capellino for fashion conscious men and women.

ST IVES BAKERY

—

Bakery

Corner of Fore Street & The Digey, St Ives, TR26 1HR
01736 798 888

On the busy corner of Fore Street, a quaint cobbled path in central St Ives, you will find this charming neighborhood bakery. Independently owned and run, St Ives Bakery offers unique products unlike many of the larger chain shops.

The windows are piled high with decadent meringues and rustic farmhouse loaves and a warm yeasty scent wafts out onto the street tempting passers-by. Many of the area's top restaurants use their breads and pastries in house.

Buy a hand-crimped pasty with flavoursome steak and perfectly crumbly shortcrust pastry, straight out of the oven if you are lucky, and head down to the beach to enjoy your comforting Cornish snack. Beware though, seagulls are prone to swoop down for a bite.

PORTHMINSTER CAFÉ

—

Restaurant

Porthminster Beach, St Ives, TR26 2EB
01736 795 352
porthminstercafe.co.uk

Perfectly located on the seafront at St Ives is the celebrated Porthminster Café. Though the décor is basic, the food excites, and the kitchen makes good use of the fresh seafood which is so accessible to them.

Head Chef Ryan Venning has worked in many top kitchens across Cornwall before settling at Porthminster Café in 2012. A favourite from the menu is the crab ravioli, which is presented in a whole crustacean shell.

The cookbook is often sold out but you can buy it online in order to recreate the dishes at home. Their second restaurant, Porthminster Kitchen is located in the heart of the town; it offers a similar cuisine highlighting flavoursome local produce.

LEACH POTTERY

—

Museum

Higher Stennack, St Ives, TR26 2HE
01736 799 703
leachpottery.com

St Ives is a famously artistic area of Britain with a long list of influential painters and potters making their home here. Founded in 1920 by Bernard Leach and Shoji Hamada as a place for potters to train and learn their trade, Leach Pottery is one of the most famous ceramic institutions in the UK.

Today, the pottery continues to operate as a working studio with the museum and gallery offering an insight into its history. The exhibition space presents the work of international and local potters, with occasional residencies from celebrated artists from around the world.

There is also a shop on site where you can purchase a cup, bowl or teapot from the Leach Standard Ware range.

THE MINACK THEATRE

—

Theatre

Porthcurno, TR19 6JU
01736 810 181
minack.com

Concealed within the scenic cliffs of Porthcurno is the enchanting Minack Theatre. The project was imagined and built by Rowena Cade, who lived in Minack House nearby. From 1931 Rowena and her gardener tirelessly moved boulders to create a space for actors to perform, and tiered steps to accommodate spectators. The first production, a version of The Tempest, was performed in this curious venue in 1932 and the theatre is still very much in use during the warmer months.

With the turquoise waters lapping in the background, it is a dramatic and magical setting to witness any play. You can also visit during the day when the theatre and museum are open to inspire and educate.

THE SHORE

—

Restaurant

13/14 Alverton Street, Penzance, TR18 2QP
01736 362 444
theshorerestaurant.uk

Bruce Rennie is one of the chefs leading the exciting, quickly evolving food scene in Penzance. After gaining experience at prestigious restaurants such as two Michelin starred Martin Wishart in Edinburgh, Bruce moved to Cornwall to head up the kitchen at the Gurnard's Head before opening his own eatery in September 2015.

The restaurant, which occupies the Old Buttery, is decorated in muted shades with seaside motifs. Although there are no sea views, Bruce more than compensates with the flavoursome and creative plates of food. His dishes showcase the fishermen's daily catch and champion ingredients which the area produces in abundance. The lunch menu is extremely reasonable, a taste of fine dining in a modest seaside dining room.

NO. 56

—

Shop

14 Chapel Street, Penzance, TR18 4AW
01736 366 293
no-56.com

Chapel Street in Penzance is a shopper's paradise with an assortment of unique design and retro outlets. On a Saturday afternoon it is a lovely lane to explore, stopping at each shop to rummage through the vintage trinkets or peruse the desirable objects and garments.

After a career in mens and womenswear design, Carole Elsworth set up No. 56 where she uses her experience to put together a personal collection based on natural materials and simple designs. The shop has a fine assortment of stationery and homeware, displayed in a fresh minimalist setting. Pick up a bottle of J Herbin violet-scented ink, a couple of beeswax candles or a Peter Swanson ceramic pouring bowl. Carole is constantly expanding the range to include her latest favourite finds, from Cornwall and further afield.

CHAPEL HOUSE

—

Hotel

Chapel Street, Penzance, TR18 4AQ
01736 362 024
chapelhousepz.co.uk

This beautiful, restored townhouse is on the corner of Chapel Street, one of Penzance's most picturesque roads. With views overlooking the sea and St Michael's Mount, it is in an enviable position. Owner Susan Stuart saw an opportunity to renovate and refresh this grand historic building, previously the home of the Penzance Arts Club, offering Penzance visitors a serene and luxurious place to stay.

The boutique hotel has six double bedrooms to choose from and each is thoughtfully designed with a mix of antique pieces and modern amenities. Reclaimed 1930s office lamps frame the bespoke beds, and a mini ipad in each room allows you to facetime for room service should you need it. Room 2 is particularly beautiful with an Ashton & Bentley bathtub and lots of natural light. Wherever possible, Susan supports local makers and suppliers; toiletries are sourced from Penzance beauty brand, Pure Nuff Stuff, and the artwork on the walls is loaned from Newlyn School of Art. Susan's delicious breakfasts and dinners are enjoyed in the communal dining room, where you can also find wellies for muddy walks and blankets to borrow on chillier days.

JUBILEE POOL

—

Lido

Promenade, Penzance, TR18 4UU
01736 369 224
jubileepool.co.uk

Recently restored to its former glory, the Jubilee Pool is once again the pride of Penzance. It was originally designed by Captain F. Latham in the early 1930s and the unique Art Deco shape is said to complement the behaviour of the surrounding waves. Where possible original details have been kept, notably the welcoming 'Bathing Pool' sign and the cubist influenced changing rooms.

Surprisingly, the Jubilee is one of the only remaining saltwater tidal pools left in Europe. The main pool is suitable for all swimmers, whilst a smaller pool accommodates young children.

A relaxed café at the poolside is a welcome addition for athletic visitors needing sustenance or a refreshing drink. The lido is a glorious spot for summer swims or family picnics, and the brilliant blue pools are a beautiful addition to the Penzance shore.

TREMENHEERE SCULPTURE GARDENS

—

Gardens

near Gulval, Penzance, TR20 8YL
01736 448 089
tremenheere.co.uk

This vast and verdant garden in Penzance is definitely not just for art enthusiasts; the route through the epic plants and trees will transport you from the moment you step inside. A short drive from the town, Tremenheere is a dramatic setting for impressive sculptural works both permanent and temporary. The unique positioning and climate allows exotic plants and flowers to flourish, creating a tropical world. From the top of the hill there are magical vistas of St Michael's Mount and the coastline.

Renowned artists such as David Nash and Tim Shaw have interacted with the landscape to create specific works which complement the setting, but James Turrell's Skyspace (Tewlwolow Kernow) is perhaps the most mesmerising work, an oval space showing the ever-changing sky. After exploring the gardens, visit Tremenheere Kitchen for wholesome food and the shop, Artisan, has a small selection of thoughtful gifts.

ORIGIN COFFEE ROASTERS, HARBOUR HEAD

—

Café

Harbour Head, Porthleven, TR13 9JY
origincoffee.co.uk

Established in 2004 by a group of enthusiasts, Origin specialises in sourcing and roasting exceptional coffee. The company was founded in Cornwall and their Roastery in Helston is available for tours, with prior booking.

In 2013 Origin coffee opened a café at Harbour Head in Porthleven, supplying locals with high quality coffee and a cool, contemporary place to enjoy it. On a quiet afternoon in this sleepy seaside town Origin is the perfect place to enjoy the views with one of their speciality blends and a slice of artisan cake. Due to its popularity, Origin has also set up shop in London, with cafés in Shoreditch, Hammersmith and an outpost in The British Library.

Please mind
the step

KESTLE BARTON

—

Gallery

Manaccan, Helston, TR12 6HU
01326 231 811
kestlebarton.co.uk

Hidden away in the depths of the Helston countryside, Kestle Barton is a visionary, multi-purpose creative space.

This ancient Cornish farmstead opened in 2010 following a full restoration and the beautiful old buildings now house a boutique gallery, as well as guest rooms. Surrounded by colourful, flower filled meadows, it is an idyllic place to spend an afternoon perusing the artwork and wandering around the gardens. Art installations showcase the work of Cornish artists and those from further afield.

During warmer months special events make use of the venue, including seed garden workshops, camping experiences and a 'lazy luncheon' series, which complement the enchanting dwelling.

FINISTERRE

—

Shop

19 High Street, Falmouth, TR11 2AB
01326 318 482
finisterre.com

Tom Kay founded Finisterre in 2002 with the aim of providing surfers with a technical clothing range to wear before and after surfing. The brand has since grown at speed, and there are now four stores, including a flagship shop in London.

The quintessentially Cornish collection utilises high quality materials that provide warmth and functionality. Finisterre supports local responsibly sourced fabrics and factories, and many of the garments use Merino wool from the very special British Bowmont Merino sheep based in Devon. Whilst much of the gear is focused on action sportswear and accessories, Finisterre also offers a selection of knitwear and clothes with a classic coastal aesthetic.

TORO

—

Shop

Old Brewery Yard, High Street, Falmouth, TR11 2BY
07528 562 737
toro-studio.com

Falmouth is a city of creatives and has spawned many inventive projects and businesses. Toro is found in the Old Brewery Yard, amongst a number of artistic boutiques - it is a tiny and cute studio crowded with whimsical hanging plants and shelves of cacti. The plants look at home on the attractive wood furniture in the shop, all created by local designer, Heather Scott. Toro owner, Victoria May Harrison, believes plants have the power to change the dynamics of a space, adding character while lifting the mood.

Pick a plant or choose from Toro's range of Honest skincare and candles in suitably green flavours like Eucalyptus Leaf. To keep your succulents healthy ask Victoria for advice on how to water and nurture them.

ESPRESSINI

—

Café

39 Killigrew St, Falmouth, TR11 3PW
espressini.co.uk

There are more and more promising independent coffee shops in Cornwall; Espressini on Killigrew Street in Falmouth is one of the best. This characterful venue serves a bespoke blend of beans sourced and roasted by Yallah Coffee, selected specially for them from growers around the world. Inside, the café is cosy and familiar with mismatched antique furniture, and the chatter accompanied by a thoughtful playlist. The coffee is bold in flavour and served to your preference. Brunch is particularly popular with a menu of tempting and indulgent dishes displaying a wide range of influences from world cuisines.

Nearby, on Falmouth harbour, is Dulce, the smaller sibling of Espressini which, as well as offering freshly brewed coffee, sells equipment to help you make the perfect cup at home.

FOLKLORE

—

Shop

Old Brewery Yard, High Street, Falmouth, TR11 2BY
folklorefalmouth.co.uk

Folklore is tucked away in Falmouth's Old Brewery Yard, a courtyard full of creative businesses. It is a serene and beautiful store stocking a carefully curated range of functional and aesthetic products from young local designers.

The shop presents a variety of handcrafted objects such as quirky ceramics by Hannah Lawrence, contemporary woodwork by Felix McCormack and delicate jewellery by Ellie Hughes. Sarah Johnson's hand-dyed indigo smocks are both unique and wearable, and inventive recycled bags are a boyish addition by Francli.

Despite its limited size, the shop has enough stock to keep visitors intrigued, especially if you are keen to hear the story behind each desirable item. The collection is constantly evolving as the makers are inspired by their Cornish surroundings to make new works.

POTAGER GARDEN

—

Restaurant & Café

High Cross, Constantine, Falmouth, TR11 5RF
01326 341 258
potagergarden.org

Nestling in the enchanting Constantine countryside, Potager Garden is a lovely place to spend time, indulging in a healthy vegetarian feast in the greenhouse or a refreshing drink in the sunshine outside. This daytime café was previously an abandoned plant nursery before it was transformed into a picturesque haven for eating and relaxing. Chef Awen McBride uses organic produce from the gardens and all the bread and ice-cream is handmade in house.

Six studios on site are used by resident artists, and frequent Open Studio days allow the public to view the work for free. The gardens are constantly evolving, with a wealth of beautiful flowers and interesting foliage, so it is always a rewarding place to visit.

NANCARROW

—

Farm

Zelah, near Truro, TR4 9DQ
01872 540 343
nancarrowfarm.co.uk

The feast nights at Nancarrow Farm have become renowned across West Cornwall; popular with locals and visitors, they sell out fast. Primarily a family-run farm, the scenic 100-acre grounds produce an abundance of high quality organic meats. For nine generations the farmers, their family and friends have eaten around the kitchen table enjoying hearty home cooked dishes and homebrewed Barn Ale. With a new professional kitchen on site, the team is now able to welcome guests to memorable events, private cookery workshops and exciting feast nights.

Each month a new menu is designed around the farm's own produce; everything is cooked in a wood-fired oven with live music providing an atmospheric accompaniment. There are also eight charming en-suite bedrooms and tipis in the orchard for guests to book, if staying over.

TREGOTHNAN

—

Gardens

The Woodyard, Tresillian, Truro, TR2 4AJ
01872 520 000
tregothnan.co.uk

Supplying some of Britain's most prestigious tearooms, Tregothnan is a stalwart example of a fine English brand. Home to the Boscawen family since 1334, this is where the first English tea in the UK was planted as recently as 1999. The extensive, manicured gardens are home to a variety of interesting exotic plants and a thriving Camellia sinensis tea crop. The heritage site and gardens are only accessible to guests if a guided tour is booked.

After a bracing walk, afternoon tea can be provided in the house, accompanied, of course by Tregothan tea in a range of flavours. This luxurious tea can be found in celebrated hotels and tearooms across the country, including Fortnum & Mason and The Savoy.

DRIFTWOOD

—

Hotel & Restaurant

Rosevine, Portscatho, St Mawes, TR2 5EW
01872 580 644
driftwoodhotel.co.uk

Driftwood has dramatic sea views and its own private beach and is set amongst acres of lush green gardens, just a short drive from St Mawes. The classic bedrooms are decorated in a fresh seaside style, with striped materials and beach themed features.

The hotel's Michelin star restaurant is reason alone to visit Driftwood. It is open just for adults, and only in the evenings when chef Chris Eden creates impeccable dishes, showcasing the best local produce with innovation and flair. The menu changes regularly though a favourite, like the striking 'Thunder and Lightning Tart' with saffron jelly and ginger beer, is a firm fixture.

For lunch, order a filled picnic basket to enjoy after a walk on the beach. Hidden Hut is another dining option nearby, a secretive café with a wholesome menu.

HOTEL TRESANTON

—

Hotel

27 Lower Castle Rd, St Mawes, TR2 5DR
01326 270 055
tresanton.com

Tresanton was the first design conscious hotel in Cornwall and is a favourite for many sojourning in the South West. It is located on the sea's edge, in the quaint fishing village of St Mawes, and guests can enjoy spectacular views from every room.

Owned and designed by the illustrious Olga Polizzi, the space evokes her personality and style in even the smallest details. Bedrooms feature an eclectic mix of vintage furniture and luxurious nautically themed fabrics, whilst the modern bistro is a relaxed place to spend time.

Don't miss a trip out on the hotel's famed Pinuccia, an immaculately restored 1930s sailing boat. This classic yacht is beautiful enough on still waters, but on a windy day is a real Cornish coastal experience.

THE IDLE ROCKS

—

Hotel

Harbourside, St Mawes, TR2 5AN
01326 270 270
idlerocks.com

Dramatically placed on the edge of the rocks at St Mawes, this stylish hotel offers a luxurious seaside experience. The characterful building is over a century old, starting life as a bakery before being transformed into a coastal hotel in the 1930s. The current owners, David and Karen Richards, purchased the hotel in 2010, and completed a transformative makeover in 2012.

Each of the nineteen rooms has been individually designed by Karen to complement the nautical surroundings and the common areas showcase captivating Cornish art. The hotel's restaurant is headed up by Guy Owen who serves modern culinary delights making it a destination eatery in the area. For top tips on where to eat, shop and swim, speak to Sid, the hotel's in-the-know concierge.

ISLES OF SCILLY

—

Escape

Isles of Scilly, TR24 0QQ
01720 422 849
tresco.co.uk

Those in the know about British travel, take an annual pilgrimage to the Isles of Scilly. Of the 1500 or so islands in the archipelago only five are inhabited and after a short flight with Isles of Scilly Travel from the mainland to St Mary's, the other islands are accessible by boat just ten minutes or less apart. The serene waters and warm climate provide an idyllic retreat for visitors and a safe, quiet lifestyle for the islanders.

Choose an island destination dependent on what you desire from a holiday, Tresco for luxurious bliss, Bryher for a rugged remote escape or St Agnes for an isolated artistic retreat. Accommodation varies from campsites to rented seaview cottages, or for something extra special book in to Hell Bay Hotel. Local restaurants celebrate the produce from the surrounding ocean, communal feasting at Crab Shack is not to be missed. There are plenty of sea-based activities to amuse, and on land the Tresco Abbey Gardens are the most visited attraction. With hundreds of exotic plants, flowers and trees carefully selected from all over the world and immaculately nurtured, it is quite a spectacle, especially when the sun shines.

OLGA POLIZZI
—
HOTELIER & DESIGNER

Olga Polizzi opened Hotel Tresanton in St Mawes in 1998, the first design hotel in Cornwall. Eldest daughter of Lord Forte, she is Director of Design at Rocco Forte Hotels, proprietors of Browns in London, the Balmoral in Edinburgh and Hotel de Russie in Rome. As well as Hotel Tresanton, Olga also owns the Grade I listed Hotel Endsleigh in Devon, and has decorated both in her inimitable style with a mix of vintage and modern treasures.

Tell us how you came to open Hotel Tresanton.
The best decision that I have ever made was ignoring everyone who told me "you can't make money in Cornwall". Granada bought Forte in 1996 and for the first time in my life I was cash-rich. To begin with, I had no idea what to do with the money.

For years, my husband, William Shawcross, had been visiting St Mawes with his parents (we still live in the house next to the hotel) and had seen what is now Tresanton in its heyday. He said that I could do something really good with it and we thought about it for two years. I would look at the wild rear garden and see the magic. The sailing is among the best in the country and the views are stunning.

Once we had finally decided that I should do it, the work began. Everything needed to be redone. The old hotel had been considered smart in its day, but tastes had changed. The rebuilding took only ten months in the end, but that was with a lot of hard work.

Tresanton was the best thing I ever did. Although I had been around hotels and working in hotels all my life, Tresanton was the first time I could really do everything the way I wanted it. I did not have a specific vision, I just knew I wanted it to be a simple, smart, seaside hotel. I chose everything of the best quality, like the

biggest baths I could find, so the guests would enjoy the experience.

Which is your favourite room at Hotel Tresanton and why?
The Lamorran suite sits above the main Tresanton building, so the views of St Mawes Bay and beyond are even more spectacular. You are cocooned in your own apartment with three bedrooms, two big bathrooms and a large sitting room. Every room has a door onto a private terrace and it's a lovely vista of sailing boats of all sizes.

The suite is perfect for a family with three or four children and was conceived with that in mind. One of the bedrooms is smart and light-filled, the other is like a ship's cabin with two built-in bunks and its own large television set into the wall... heaven for any child.

There are washed wooden floors throughout and a casual marine feel in keeping with the rest of Tresanton. The furniture is a mix of old and new, with some unusual pieces, and some of the best local art.

Tresanton has its own sailing yacht, Pinuccia. Is sailing a passion of yours?
You wouldn't know it but I'm very good at sailing. I fill in wherever needed, needless to say I'm not the captain.

Where is home?

London. The centre of the universe! A small house with a little garden near Marble Arch and Hyde Park. I can walk to Paddington Station so feel slightly closer to Cornwall when I'm there.

What do you think makes Cornwall special?

Being surrounded by water on three sides gives the light a very special quality, almost magical. Cornwall is well known for attracting artists for this reason. The air that you breathe has blown across the Atlantic Ocean so is extremely fresh.

Where are your favourite places to go in Cornwall?

There are wonderful things to see. I love the Lizard Peninsula, because it's so mysterious and slightly spooky. St Ives is full of good art galleries: I visit the Barbara Hepworth Museum and Sculpture Garden time and time again. Newlyn Art Gallery shows young Cornish artists, and Truro has Lemon Street Gallery, which sells contemporary art. There are great places to eat, too. The Hidden Hut on Porthcurnick Beach throws pop-up feast nights and if you don't book tickets in the first half hour they're on sale, you miss out.

How have you seen Cornwall change over the last ten years?

I can think of twenty restaurants in Cornwall which really are as good as anything you could find elsewhere. When we opened it was only Rick Stein on the north coast. That indicates how Cornwall has changed to now appeal to visitors from all over the world.

Who is your greatest inspiration – in work and in life?

In terms of brilliance it must be Philippe Starck, who started off the design mania in hotels. I certainly don't follow what he does per se, but he gave us the chance to see hotels in a different way. And of course my father Lord Forte.

Where do you love to shop (for antiques)? And what do you look for in particular?

I'd choose the Sablon in Brussels. It has the best antiques and design shopping in Europe – I buy quite a lot for the hotels there. Michel Lambrecht in particular is fantastic; mainly 20th century but he makes a lot of his own things; he'll buy old railings and turn them into lamps.

If you could wake up at one hotel in the world, which would it be and why?

The Hotel de Russie is spectacular - it has the most peaceful and romantic garden right in the centre of Rome, a complete oasis in the bustling city. Aside from our hotels, I like Il Pelicano in Porto Ercole.

Where would you like to travel to next?

South America, as my daughters are always threatening to go and live there – otherwise I would like to travel around Italy which I believe is the most beautiful country in the world with some of the most stunning and unexpected things to see, not to mention the food and wine.

Are there any destinations that have surprised you?

Transylvania in Romania – I would love to go back. It was wonderful walking through the flower-strewn meadows with herds of horses and flocks of sheep, and passing through small villages which take you back hundreds of years.

What memorable things have you collected from your travels?

When I travel to Verdura, our resort in Sicily, I always bring the delicious local olives and almonds home with me, as well as a piece of unusual pottery from nearby Sciacca.

NATHAN OUTLAW
—
CHEF

Nathan Outlaw began cooking as a child with his chef father, before continuing into formal food training. After working extensively with Rick Stein and Paul Ripley in Cornwall, he fell in love with Cornish produce, especially the fish. In 2003 he opened his first solo venture, The Black Pig, for which he received a Michelin star, aged just 25. He went on to establish two restaurants in Port Isaac, Restaurant Nathan Outlaw (RNO), recognised as the only two star fish restaurant in the world, and the more relaxed Outlaw's Fish Kitchen. He also has eateries in London and Dubai, and runs The Mariners Public House in Rock.

What's your story? Why Cornwall?
I grew up in Kent but came on holiday to Cornwall as a child every year. I first came to live and work here aged 19. I had been working in London as a young commis and in every restaurant I seemed to gravitate towards the fish station, and soon decided I wanted to concentrate on fish. Rick Stein was the fish god so I came down to Cornwall to work for him and fell in love with it. In Stein's restaurant I met my wife over the hot plate, a local girl who was working front of house. I spent two years working for Rick, which included a whole year just prepping seafood (like a fishmonger). Over my time there Stein had become huge and Padstow was no longer a sleepy fishing town.

I loved Cornwall but needed more experience so moved to Lords of the Manor Hotel in the Cotswolds and then the Vineyard at Stockcross, in both working for John Campbell, a very good Michelin starred chef. Before long I came back to Cornwall and opened my first restaurant, the Black Pig in 2003. With just me in the kitchen, at only 25 years old, it was very hard work. I never knew much about Michelin stars... but after eight months the Black Pig was awarded one.

I then went on to open my fine dining restaurant and fish kitchen, both in Port Isaac. Everything in my restaurants is inspired by the sea and local produce.

You've also got your London restaurant... how do you cater differently there?
My London restaurant has been open nearly four years and initially was very different. It is all fish at RNO and London is the same, but in London the fish is delivered from the sea six or seven hours later. We've got a very efficient transfer – the fish goes on to the train at Penzance, straight to Paddington where it is picked up by electric cars to take it to the restaurant. I know the fishermen, and I know exactly where it comes from so I'm confident that it's the best fish in London. Tom, the head chef there, has been with me for seven years... he is very Cornish and is brilliant.

How have you seen Cornwall change in the time you've been here?
It's changed in a big way. Some Cornish people may not agree, but I think Rick had a massive effect on the county. He brought awareness that there are amazing ingredients and food here. When I first came, there wasn't the variety there is now. You can eat really well all over Cornwall, there's a great Asian restaurant in Newquay (called Kahuna) and a street food place in Truro which is fantastic – the reason they are so good is because the owners have travelled the world surfing and eating in all these different countries, so they know how to make authentic food. The pubs have improved a lot too – they've had to up their game because of everything else around them.

Cornwall has become a foodie destination, and we've noticed that a large number of our customers visit as part of a foodie tour, trying different cuisines all around the county.

Are there any up and coming chefs or restaurants that you're particularly excited about?
Andy Appleton's at Trevibban Mill Vineyard and Tom Adams at Coombeshead Farm are the two most exciting recent openings in Cornwall. The Shore in Penzance is also great and Porthminster Café has a lovely location with amazing views.

You said your style is based on the sea... how do you define it?
Probably the one thing is... I'm always looking to take things away from a plate. When you're a young chef you're trying to show all your skills, but for me it's more about getting the best out of the ingredients. The guys we use for vegetables (a father and son) are not specialists in micro herbs or anything fancy, but they grow proper onions and carrots, which make a huge difference in the depth of flavour compared to a sack of regular onions. If you eat something that's been done properly you'll notice it, the simplest dishes can blow you away.

In France or Italy, you can go to a market and you buy better produce than they serve in a restaurant. There's no excuse for bad food. The tomatoes we get are from Rob Hocking at Buttervilla Growers near Looe, he doesn't produce as much as other growers because he prunes the vines; he goes for quality and the flavour is so incredible. When I started I said to Chris (head chef at RNO) I want to get to the point where I could just put a great piece of fish and sauce on a plate, he laughed and said you can't do that, but now we do...

Is there a fish that you think is underrated? Or you'd like to use more...
There's fish I'd like to use that I don't. I love octopus for example, but I can't get it from the sea here in Cornwall. We use it in the fish kitchen and the pub, but RNO only uses fish indigenous to this area. The octopus here is single sucker and is tough, you don't get tender Mediterranean octopus. That's a bit frustrating. We haven't got any tuna either for the same reasons.

Things like cuttlefish are great when it's in season, but it's rarely cooked right (either over or undercooked) but Japanese chefs know how to use it.

If you could have one meal anywhere... where would you have it?
There's a restaurant I haven't been to but I really want to try, Asador Etxebarri, a grill restaurant in San Sebastian. I've been to San Sebastian twice, the first time I visited all the 3* restaurants and on the second trip I properly discovered the little tapas and pintxos bars. The fine dining restaurants don't capture where you are, but the bars are outstanding. We spent four nights in a row doing a tapas bar crawl... everywhere you look you worry you've missed somewhere and you want to try more. There's one in particular (Ganbara), which is packed shoulder to shoulder, the diners spill out onto the street, eating spider crab tarts, plates of porcini with raw egg yolks, little prawns and anchovies, and great wine...

And finally... if you were on a desert island and only allowed three ingredients, what would you have?
I could catch my own fish and harvest my own salt... that's two of the most important things. I could probably make vinegar too. I think good oils are so important, more than butter, so that would be my first luxury. I'm obsessed with marmite so I'd definitely take that. I could try to cook it with fish and after a while I'm sure I'd come up with a recipe... and last thing, I think probably cheese, good cheese.

TOM RAFFIELD

DESIGNER

Tom Raffield has made Cornwall his home, setting up his successful wood-bending business in the woodland around Helston. Originally from Exmoor, Tom moved to Cornwall permanently after studying at Falmouth School of Art. After experimenting extensively with steam-bending he founded his own company, creating innovative and inspiring furniture. His range of sculptural lighting ornaments and design focused pieces aim to be 'beautiful in form and practical in function'. Utilising the natural habitat, Tom and his team use materials from the woodland that surrounds the workshop, creating objects in a consciously sustainable way. His range can be seen in both commercial and domestic settings and the natural, organic shapes are versatile enough to suit any environment.

You aren't from Cornwall originally but studied at Falmouth School of Art. What was your first impression of Cornwall?
I fell in love with it; it is about as far away from England (culturally and geographically!) as you can get without going to another country. The nautical and artistic heritage you can immerse yourself in when you live here makes it impossible to leave. The beaches, the harbours, the sea; I knew straight away this is where I wanted to live and study. The land and seascape together with the dramatic weather compound that isolated feel which I love. Being surrounded by such beauty really helps with creativity. There are also lots of talented makers down here from the boatbuilding industry, which helps us when looking for new craftsmen. In terms of bringing up a family and lifestyle, if you like the outdoors nowhere else in the UK can beat it!

So coming out of university, how did you get to where you are now?
After university two friends and I set up a design company. Our philosophy was to use green unseasoned timber and transform it into a contemporary product that was affordable. We were all conceptual and interested in the design side, but not good at business, so after two years we all decided to move on.

I moved into a shed at the end of the garden and my wife helped me set up the new business, Tom Raffield. She was very creative as a trained designer, but also good at the business side. In 2012 we bought the current land and moved my workshop here. Charlie (my first employee) and I built the work shed out of the trees on the site. Now, a few years on, there's a team of us and I can concentrate on design, which I love.

And you've designed a new home on the land as well, can you tell us about that?
The land we bought had an old Grade II listed gamekeepers lodge set amongst several acres of woodland. I wanted to build something using the resources on site so we designed an extension to the lodge. It is largely comprised of timber and rock from the site and we have tried to use as much as possible from our own woodland. We've used the steam-bending technique to create something that blends in with the landscape. Rather than joining two bits of wood, we've bent the wood for the corners of the house, which creates quite a striking aesthetic. It's also a very sustainable way of

building a house as you can use oak or ash, which both grow everywhere in England, and there's no glue. The extension has a flat roof, balconies and grass on top. The oak, which has come from the trees around it, will soon weather and grey to match the surrounding woodland.

How important is being in Cornwall for your work?

In terms of production and logistics it can be difficult, but the benefit of Cornwall, for me, is being surrounded by the seascape, woodlands and nature. It's a brilliant environment for creative projects and a lovely place to live and raise a family.

There are lots of young creatives in Cornwall... especially coming out of Falmouth Art School.

Yes, there are so many great things going on and so many people that deserve recognition because they are doing amazing things. Part of what I want to start doing is to help the next wave of young designers so that they can continue to push Cornwall forward.

Steam-bending is the main technique you employ – how did you learn about it?

It's a process that has been around since the Vikings! I started using it at university and later began to develop my own process and do my own thing. You don't need high-tech systems or machines, and once you understand how it works and can control the variables the scope becomes huge. It's a beautiful process; wood is always going to be fashionable, and bent wood - whether for furniture, houses or lights - is just a way of manipulating timber into different forms. It's also very sustainable, because it's just local timber and water.

Lots of other people are very good at steam-bending but use it to make the same products repeatedly. For me, I wasn't ever really taught how to steam-bend so I came to it organically and with no set rules. It's about being creative, trying to do something different and having fun with the design and materials that I use.

Tell us about your design style and vision.

Craftsmanship, sustainability and innovation; these are the three key ingredients prevalent in each one of our products. Everything we do stands for these qualities and this is what helps our work stand out from other competing mass produced products.

"Inspired by nature shaped by hand"... this is a statement we often use and feel is synonymous with our brand. We look to nature and our surroundings for inspiration.

What is normally the starting point for a new design?

I design through making so never sit on a computer designing but always start with making small wooden or wire models before moving straight into steam-bending. As we make all of our pieces ourselves, understanding the constraints and potential of the processes we use is integral to product development. Also, developing new tools and ways of using the steam-bending technique is very much at the heart of many new designs.

Which designers have most influenced your approach?

Thomas Heatherwick for his ability to innovate and create buildings, products and vehicles you never thought possible. But above all, Charles and Ray Eames in terms of how they developed a wood bending technique and used it in different disciplines to show its potential.

What would be your dream commission?

A giant sculptural piece of art that was interactive in the sense that it invited people to use it and walk or sit within it. If money and time was no issue and I was given complete creative control... that would be my dream!

SID WILLIAMS

—

HOTEL CONCIERGE

Sid Williams is Cornwall's only hotel concierge. Born and raised in Cornwall, he moved to London to study art but kept a passion for his home county and a yearning to return. He fell into hospitality while in London and has never looked back. Sid is concierge at The Idle Rocks, a 19-bedroom hotel idyllically situated on the harbourside at St Mawes.

Tell us about yourself and how you came to become Cornwall's only hotel concierge.
I'm from Cornwall originally and returned here after living and working in London for twenty years. I tried all sorts of jobs – from motorcycle courier to TV autocue operator – before running the shop in The Sanderson Hotel. Living in London, I had an uncontrollable urge to always try to find the best bar or restaurant, so I quickly became good friends with the concierge and when a position came up in the team I jumped at the chance. I love exploring – if I go to a new city, within an hour I have to know where everything is!

Years later, I had a family and wanted to move back to Cornwall. I heard David Richards had bought a hotel in St Mawes so I got in contact. Concierges weren't (and still aren't) known in Cornwall – I'm the only one – but David was forward thinking and recognised the value a concierge could add to a guest's holiday. Cornwall is a big county, there are a lot of different things going on and I can save people a lot of time and make the difference to a holiday. If you've got two children and want to go surfing one day and sailing the next, or you just want a safe beach and an ice-cream, I can tell you where to go.

What question do you get asked the most?
Generally I get asked about beaches. Everyone wants to know where to find a lovely secret beach, but lots of the best secrets are kept by the Cornish and I'm not going to give it all away! I can point people in the direction of little lost coves that you can only get to by water, and we can organise for guests to be dropped off on the beach by kayak or water-taxi and picked up a few hours later. For a couple that have come down from London, to arrive and minutes later be sat on a beach on their own, with a bottle of something cold, it's special.

We get a range of guests, from families to young couples; so I offer suggestions to suit. Subtropical gardens – Glendurgan and Trelissick for example – are very popular and both stunning, and the coastal walks around the hotel are some of the best in Cornwall. Lots of people go for a short stroll and just carry on and on. Quite often we get a call from guests saying they ended up walking miles up the coast and can we pick them up!

What about the more conventional things like restaurants?
In July and August I always say to people when they arrive that it may feel quite sleepy but if you want to eat anywhere particular in the next few nights, you need to let me know and I'll make the bookings because everything gets booked up. Luckily I have a little bit of leverage with a couple of the restaurants I know.

What do you think really makes Cornwall special?

The size of Cornwall means it is a place of contrasts. Rock is very glamorous with big white beaches, the Lizard is beautiful, quiet and hidden, West Cornwall has a bit of hippy culture and then St Mawes is quite chic with great beaches and sailing and family-oriented beaches. There's so much variety and so much going on. When the sun is out, there is nowhere better to be! It's beautiful.

How have you seen Cornwall change?

When I left Cornwall in the 90s there was nothing here, there was no vibrancy but now it's transformed. There are creative and independent brands, from photography businesses to new fashion brands, these innovators are doing incredible things that just didn't exist before. There are lots of start-up businesses that are using experience and influences gained elsewhere. On the other hand, companies like Finisterre are local guys from St Agnes who started out making t-shirts and a few jackets and now have several shops, including a branch in London.

What are some of your favourite things to do in Cornwall?

I'm from an arts background so I love the creative aspects of the county. Tremenheere Sculpture Garden in Penzance is wonderful, I particularly love the James Turrell installation. Cornwall is also full of festivals and Port Elliot is on my list every year, so is Porthleven Food Festival.

What about activities or offerings that Idle Rocks put on?

We can offer almost anything that a guest wants. We have boats, kayaks, and can even organise helicopter tours, but the most popular activity we offer is a fishing trip. You get taken out by a local fisherman and are taught to catch mackerel and lobster – it's always a big hit. Guests come back from a trip and the kitchen will then cook up their fresh catch for them to enjoy for dinner.

Where do you go on holidays?

I still like a city. I still like to smell it and see it. I recently went to Copenhagen, which was great – it's a city that works on so many levels. I also love LA, which is almost like an extreme version of Cornwall – it's a city but with beaches and deserts.

What about in the future – is there anywhere you'd really love to visit that you haven't yet?

I love sailing so probably sailing from here to the Caribbean. Otherwise, there's a hotel in Utah called Amangiri, part of the Aman Hotel group, which is quite something. It's built into a canyon and looks incredible – just staggering.

Is there anywhere in particular that you think is really exciting in Cornwall at the moment?

Porthleven still isn't fully on the tourist map but has great restaurants that are mostly frequented by locals. And the coastline there is stunning. Also on the north coast, St Agnes doesn't get too busy and there are lots of great beaches, restaurants and pubs.

We know you won't want to give away all your secrets, but do you have one gem you're willing to tell...

I'll give you one... Genki in St Agnes, is a café run by a local guy who lived in Japan for a long time and they do great sushi nights. It's a beauty.

And lastly, are there any artists or designers that we should know about?

Lemon Street Gallery in Truro is one of my favourites. They have a contemporary list of artists and the owner also has her own private "by appointment only" sculpture garden at her house.

FURTHER IDEAS

—

2 FORE STREET
Restaurant
2 Fore Street, Mousehole, Penzance, TR19 6QU
01736 731 164
2forestreet.co.uk

THE ART OF WINE
Shop
7 Nalder's Court, Truro, TR1 2XH
01872 270 032
theartofwine.co.uk

BEN'S CORNISH KITCHEN
Restaurant
West End, Marazion, Penzance, TR17 0EL
01736 719 200
benscornishkitchen.com

HIDDEN HUT
Café
Porthcurnick Beach, Rosevine (near Portscatho),
St Mawes, TR2 5HD
hiddenhut.co.uk

THE LOST GARDENS OF HELIGAN
Gardens
Pentewan, St Austell, PL26 6EN
01726 845 100
heligan.com

PRAWN ON THE LAWN
Restaurant
11 Duke Street, Padstow, PL28 8AB
01841 532 223
prawnonthelawn.com

STEIN'S FISHERIES & SEAFOOD BAR
Restaurant
South Quay, Padstow, PL28 8BL
01841 532 700
rickstein.com

STRONG ADOLFOS
Café
Hawksfield, A39, Wadebridge, (near Padstow), PL27 7LR
01208 816 949
strongadolfos.com

WILD FAL
Escape
The Charcoal Cottage, Tolcarne Woods, St Just-In-Roseland,
(near St Mawes), TR2 5JH
wildfal.co.uk

YALLAH COFFEE
Roastery
Argal Home Farm, Kergilliack, Falmouth, TR11 5PD
01326 727 383
yallahcoffee.co.uk

WEEKEND JOURNALS

Editor: Milly Kenny-Ryder
thoroughlymodernmilly.com

Designer: Simon Lovell

Photographer: Gabriel Kenny-Ryder
gabrielkennyryder.com

All venues have been visited personally.

Many thanks to Granny Green for her hospitality and
Chris Kenny for his invaluable creative opinion.

First published in the United Kingdom in 2016 by Weekend Journals Ltd.

Printed on FSC approved uncoated paper
ISBN: 978-1-5272-0086-9

hello@weekendjournals.co.uk
weekendjournals.co.uk